ACE Mathematics Games 5

14 exciting blackline activities to engage ages 9-10

David Smith

3. **Introduction**

4. **Hexums**
   recall and use facts for
   multiplication tables up to 12 x 12

7. **Square Up**
   recall and use facts for
   multiplication tables up to 12 x 12

10. **Total Tables**
    recall and use facts for
    multiplication tables up to 12 x 12

13. **Multiple Madness**
    identify multiples and factors of
    numbers up to 100

15. **Hooked!**
    count forwards and backwards with positive
    and negative whole numbers, including
    through zero

17. **Dare!**
    add and subtract numbers to
    one decimal place

19. **Speed Seekers**
    add and subtract numbers to
    one decimal place

21. **The Ten Dash**
    add and subtract numbers to
    one decimal place

23. **Battle Squares**
    divide by 10 and add and subtract three-digit
    numbers up to 1000

26. **Flamingo Bingo**
    use a range of efficient mental methods with
    numbers up to 50

30. **End of the Line**
    use a range of efficient mental methods with
    numbers up to 100

32. **Cover Up**
    use a range of efficient mental methods with
    numbers up to 100

34. **Quads**
    use a range of efficient mental methods with
    numbers up to 1000 and to
    one decimal place

36. **Monster Mash-Up!**
    use a range of efficient mental methods with
    numbers up to 1 000 000 and to
    two decimal places

TarquinGroup
www.tarquingroup.com

Acknowledgements

Thanks are due to many people but especially to my lovely wife and also my dear mum who between them patiently played all the games with me to test their initial suitability. I also have to thank the teachers and children of Peel Park Primary School for giving them a road test, spotting my errors and making suggestions on how they could be further developed and improved. Finally thanks go to the staff at Tarquin, for their support in the editing process.

Dedication

This book is dedicated to the memory of Maxine Firth, an inspirational friend and colleague who shared my ideal of an enjoyment of mathematics for all.

Published by Tarquin Publications
Suite 74, 17 Holywell Hill
St Albans
AL1 1DT

www.tarquingroup.com

Copyright © David Smith, 2014
ISBN: 978-1-907-55089-8

Printed and Distributed in the USA by IPG Books
www.ipgbook.com
www.amazon.com & major retailers

Distributed in Australia by OLM www.lat-olm.com.au

Designed in the United Kingdom

Introduction

'… practise mental calculations with increasingly large numbers to aid fluency … and mentally add and subtract tenths.'

Upper Key Stage 2 National Curriculum Programme of Study

'The teacher created a positive climate for learning in which pupils were interested and engaged.'

OFSTED Inspector

Welcome to a world of mathematical fun and games!

Easy to play and requiring only basic equipment, these educational games engage even the most reluctant of learners whilst boosting confidence for all.

Great for teachers, intervention workers, teaching assistants, private tutors and parents, the flexible nature of this game pack offers:

▶ practice for specific objectives from the new National Curriculum

▶ a great resource to:
   "ensure students are engaged in learning and generate high levels of commitment to learning"
        (Outstanding Grade Descriptors, *Ofsted School Inspection Handbook* (updated 2014))

▶ the opportunity to demonstrate a commitment to:
   "the social development of pupils at the school" within curriculum time
                    (Ofsted Framework for School Inspection (updated 2014))

▶ an effective assessment tool

▶ the promotion of problem solving and thinking skills through game strategy

▶ fun homework activities

Playing Information

All these games require a pack of playing cards and most also need some kind of coloured counters or other objects such as beads or buttons. Suitable materials are available from Tarquin - see page 40 for details. When the picture cards are used the jack represents number eleven, the queen is number twelve and the king is thirteen. To help children remember this you may want to consider writing the actual numbers in the corners of each card.

And that's all you need to know to enjoy years of happy gaming!

David Smith

Hexums

Focus

Hexums is a game for two or three players which practices recall and use of facts for multiplication tables up to 12 x 12.

What you need

▶ Playing cards (kings removed)

▶ Counters (a different colour for each player)

▶ Hexums game board

How to play

When the kings have been removed from the pack the remaining cards are shuffled and placed in a pile, face-down and within reach of all the players. Player 1 turns over a playing card from the pack and places it face-up in front of them. They then multiply the value of the card by any number from one to twelve, as long as the matching answer is on the game board.

For example

Player 1 turns over a four so can say 4 x 6 = 24 or 4 x 9 = 36, as both of these numbers are on the game board. After saying the correct answer Player 1 can place a counter on any of the matching answers on the game board.

Player 2 then turns over a card and multiplies its value by any number from one to twelve. This time a queen is turned over so Player 2 says 12 x 3 = 36 and places a counter on the matching answer on the game board.

Players continue to take cards in turn, multiplying the value on the card by any number from one to twelve and placing counters on the board. If a player gives an incorrect answer they are not able to place a counter on that turn.

How to win

Each player has to try and make a continuous line of coloured counters on adjacent numbers from the outer ring to the inner ring of shaded hexagons, as shown in the diagram.

Rule changes / Next steps

▶ Limit the players to ten counters each to try and get a winner.

▶ To play Hexums Multiples, the value of each turned card can be multiplied by any multiple of ten up to one hundred and twenty.

▶ Record multiplication facts on paper or a whiteboard. At the end of the game use these to generate other multiplication and division facts (as below) and then test each other.

6 x 12 = 72	so	12 x 6 = 72	72 ÷ 12 = 6	and	72 ÷ 6 = 12
90 x 7 = 630	so	7 x 90 = 630	630 ÷ 7 = 90	and	630 ÷ 9 = 70

Hexums
Mixed

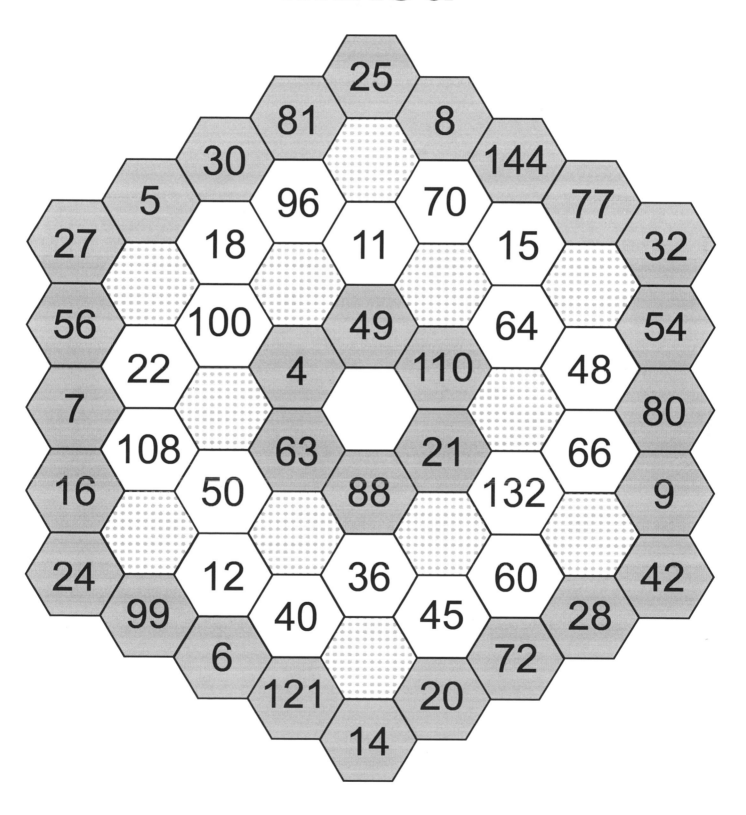

Hexums
Multiples

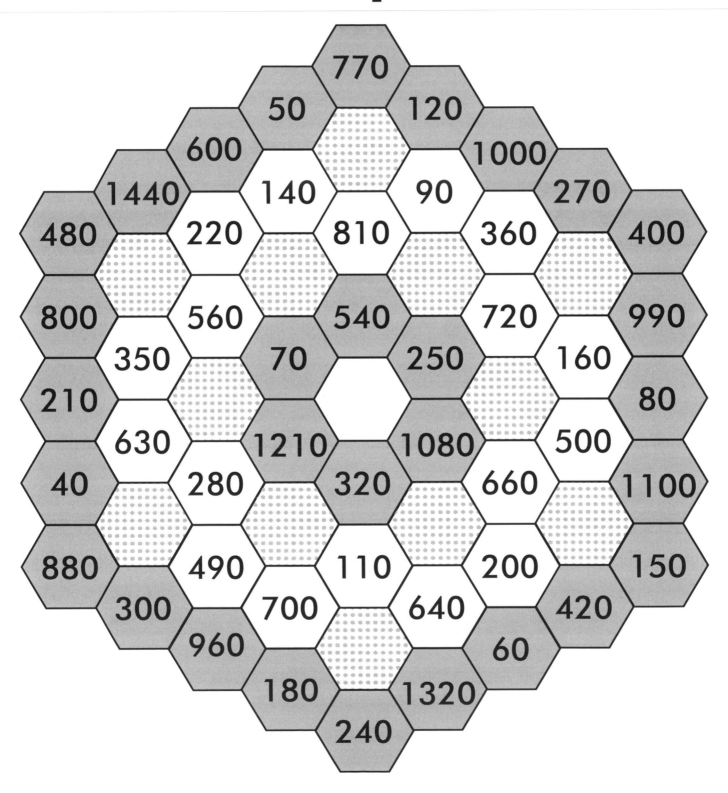

Square Up

Focus

Square Up is a game for two to four players which practices recall and use of multiplication facts for multiplication tables up to 12 x 12.

What you need

▶ Playing cards (kings removed)

▶ Counters (a different colour for each player)

▶ Square Up game board

How to play

When the kings have been removed from the pack the remaining cards are shuffled and placed in a pile, face-down and within reach of all the players. Player 1 turns over a playing card from the pack and places it face-up in front of them. The value of the card is then multiplied by any chosen number from three to twelve. The chosen calculation must have a matching answer on the game board on which the player then places their counter.

For example

Player 1 turns over an eight so could say 8 x 7 = 56, 8 x 10 = 80 or 8 x 4 = 32, since all these answers have a matching number on the game board. After saying the correct answer to their chosen calculation, Player 1 places a counter on the matching answer.

Player 2 then turns over a card and follows the same procedure. This time a seven is turned over so Player 2 says 4 x 7 = 28 and places a counter on twenty-eight on the game board.

Players continue to take cards in turn, multiply the value of the card by any number from three to twelve and place their counters on the board. If a player gives an incorrect answer they are not able to place a counter on that turn. A player may turn over another card if no matching answer can be found on the game board.

How to win

Players have to make the shape of a square, by placing counters on each corner, as shown in the diagram. The square can be any size and in any orientation; the first player to complete one is the winner.

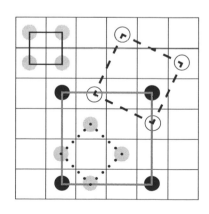

Rule changes / Next steps

▶ Play Square Up Multiples by turning a card and multiplying the value by any multiple of ten from thirty to one hundred and twenty.

▶ Players score four points for each square they make and play can continue until all their counters have been used or until there are no spaces left on the game board.

▶ Make some flashcards showing mixed multiplication or division facts on one side and the answer on the other side. Children can then use them for individual practice or to test a partner.

SQUARE UP MIXED

45	6	90	36	144	21
84	110	25	9	80	4
5	48	3	54	66	42
99	32	108	15	7	100
28	121	60	120	72	56
55	8	132	96	35	20

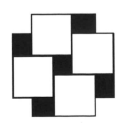

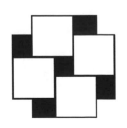

SQUARE UP MULTIPLES

540	90	1080	40	320	250
360	550	420	960	1210	720
1320	1000	560	50	900	350
800	60	280	600	80	210
150	200	1440	70	450	990
1100	480	660	840	1200	30

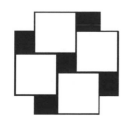 

Total Tables

Focus

Total Tables is a game for two or more players which practices recall and use of facts for multiplication tables up to 12 x 12.

What you need

▶ Playing cards (kings and aces removed)

▶ Counters (a different colour for each player)

▶ Total Tables game board

▶ Total Tables scorecard

How to play

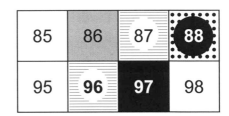

After the kings and aces have been removed from the pack, the cards are shuffled and Player 1 deals three cards to each player, placing the rest of the pack face-down within reach of all the players. Players must multiply two of their cards together, and then have the extra option of either adding or subtracting the value of the third card. Since the total of the calculation must be over fifty, players may, if necessary, multiply one of their cards by ten. So if a player had a three, a five and a nine they could then do 30 x 5 – 9 = 141.

For example

If Player 1 turns over an eight, a queen and a four, they could use them to make the following totals:

8 x 12 = 96   8 x 12 – 4 = 92   12 x 4 + 8 = 56

Placing a counter on total fifty-six or ninety-two scores thirty points for a white square, whereas placing a counter on ninety-six scores one hundred and twenty points for a striped square.

The player places their cards down, states their calculation and, if correct, places their counter on the relevant square. They then draw three new cards ready for their next turn.

Play goes to the next player and the process is repeated, with players trying to achieve the maximum number of points possible on each turn. Players should beware dotty squares, which lose them points. Each player keeps their own score using a scorecard. Players must do all their mental calculations before placing their counter and must also give a correct answer in order to do so.

Players cannot place a counter on a square that is already covered and must be ready to put their cards down when it comes to their turn. Players must place a counter unless all possible squares are covered, in which case the player cannot place a counter but draws three new cards as usual. When all the cards have been used, shuffle them and place them in a pile, face down in the middle of the table, ready for the next player's turn.

How to win

The winner of the game is the player with the most points after an agreed number of rounds.

Rule changes / Next steps

▶ Allow players to multiply the numbers on all three cards, such as 4 x 7 x 3 = 84.

▶ Remove the smaller cards to produce more difficult calculations.

Total Tables

51	**52**	53	54	**55**	56	57	**58**	59	
61	62	**63**	64	65	66	**67**	68	69	**T**
71	72	73	**74**	75	**76**	77	78	**79**	**A**
81	**82**	**83**	**84**	85	**86**	87	**88**	**89**	**B**
91	92	**93**	94	95	96	**97**	98	**99**	**L**
101	102	**103**	**104**	105	**106**	**107**	108	**109**	**E**
111	**112**	113	114	115	116	117	**118**	**119**	**S**
121	122	123	**124**	125	**126**	127	128	**129**	
131	132	**133**	**134**	135	**136**	**137**	138	139	
		T	**O**	**T**	**A**	**L**			150

Total Tables Scorecard

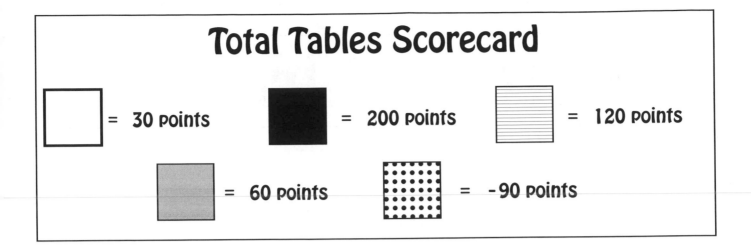

☐ = 30 points   ■ = 200 points   ▤ = 120 points

▦ = 60 points   ▨ = -90 points

Keep your score like this:

Round Number	Points for square	Total Game points
1	stripes, 120 points	120
2	dotty, -90	120 - 90 = 30
3	grey, 60	30 + 60 = 90

Round Number	Points for square	Total Game points
1		
2		
3		
4		
5		
6		
7		
8		
9		
10		
11		
12		
13		
14		
15		

Multiple Madness

Focus

Multiple Madness is a game for two or more players which practices identifying multiples and factors of numbers up to 100.

What you need

▶ Playing cards (aces to sevens)

▶ Counter

▶ Multiple Madness game board

▶ Whiteboard / paper and pen

▶ Calculator

How to play

The cards are shuffled and placed in a pile, face-down and within reach of all the players. Place a counter on the number fifty position in the middle of the game board. Player 1 takes two cards from the top of the pack and multiplies them together to get a total. That player can then move the counter the same number of places on the board by either adding or subtracting from fifty. Their choice of move depends on the number of points they can score, as follows:

For example

Player 1 picks a three and a two so they can move the counter to position fifty-six or forty-four. Fifty-six is a multiple of eight so scores eight points, whereas forty-four is a multiple of eleven so scores eleven points. Therefore, Player 1 decides to move the counter to forty-four on the game board and starts their scoring with eleven points.

Player 2 then takes two cards, multiplies them together and also adds or subtracts the total from the number under the counter on the game board. Player 2 turns over two fives so has a choice of calculating 44 + 25 = 69 or 44 − 25 = 19. Nineteen is not a multiple of any scoring number as it is a prime number so would not score any points. However, if they moved to sixty-nine on the game board they could claim three points as sixty-nine is a multiple of three.

Play continues in this fashion. Players can earn points for multiples from three up to twelve but must claim their points and explain how they know the number they have landed on is actually a multiple of that number. For example, fifty-four is a multiple of three (3 points) but the player could show that it is a multiple of nine (9 points). They can do this by saying things like 9 x 6 = 54, 54 ÷ 9 = 6 or even count up in multiples of nine to show that there really are six lots of nine in fifty-four. Their opponent can challenge an explanation and use a calculator to check whether it is correct.

Players keep a running total of their points using a whiteboard or paper and pen. This may be done by someone acting as a scorer / referee, who also decides whether player explanations are good enough to award points.

How to win

The first player to reach a total of fifty points is the winner.

Rule changes / Next steps

▶ Allow points for multiples up to fifteen, such as thirty-nine being a multiple of thirteen as 3 x 13 = 39 or sixty being a multiple of fifteen as 4 x 15 = 60. The winning total could then be raised to one hundred points.

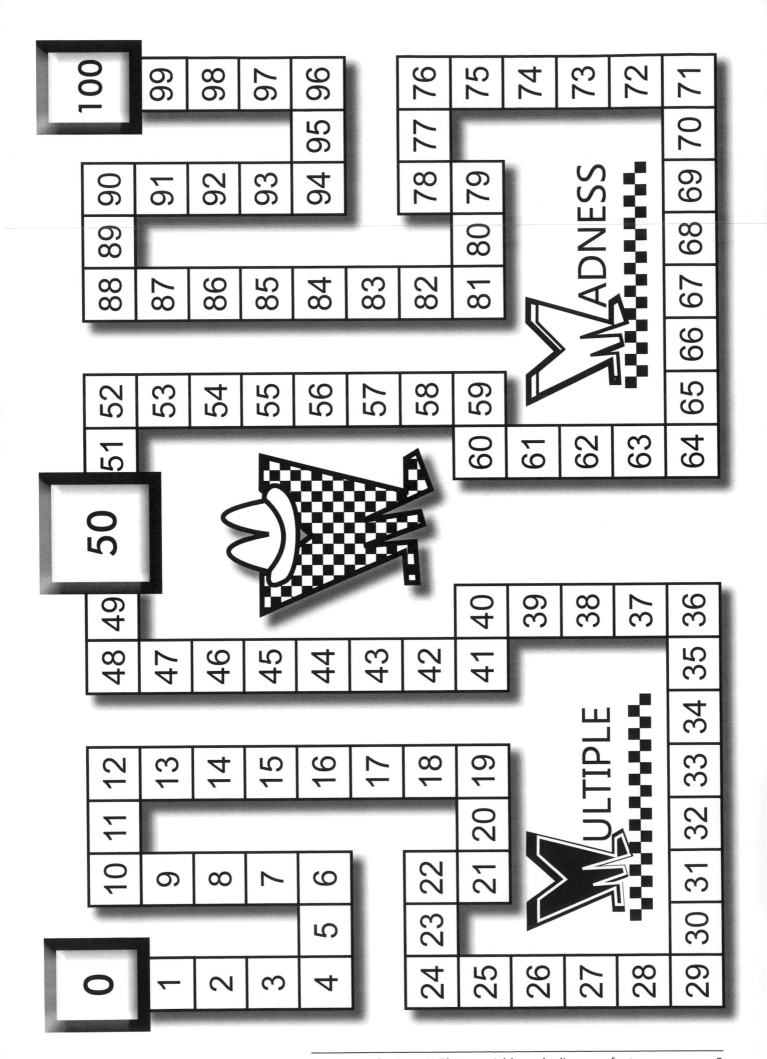

Hooked!

Focus

Hooked! is a game for two players which practices counting forwards and backwards with positive and negative whole numbers, including through zero.

What you need

▶ Playing cards

▶ Counter

▶ Hooked! game board

How to play

The cards are shuffled and placed in a pile, face-down between both players. Decide who is counting forwards and who is counting backwards. The player counting forwards moves from left to right along the game board and the player counting backwards moves from right to left. Place a counter on the middle number of the game board.

For example

Player 1 (forwards) turns over a card and adds the total to the number underneath the counter. If Player 1 turns over a six they calculate 0 + 6 = 6, and move the counter to that space on the board. If Player 1 gives an incorrect answer then the counter remains in the same place.

Player 2 (backwards) then turns over a card and subtracts its value from the number underneath the counter. So if Player 2 turns over an eight, they calculate 6 – 8 = ⁻2, and move the counter to that space on the board.

Players are encouranged to do all their mental mental calculations before moving the counter, but when crossing zero and with negative numbers they may be allowed to count the squares as they move. A correct answer must be given in order to move the counter. When all the cards have been used, shuffle them and place them back down in a pile so that play can continue.

How to win

Player 2 (subtracting) hooks the fish and wins by getting the counter to land on or go past minus fifteen whilst Player 1 (adding) hooks the fish and wins by getting the counter to land on or go past fifteen.

Rule changes / Next steps

▶ Change roles and play again so both players practice their addition and subtraction skills.

▶ Play for a set number of turns and the player who is closest to their end of the game board wins.

▶ Remove the lower cards (aces to threes) to make the game last longer and have even more calculations crossing zero.

▶ Make links between adding 6 to 8 to get 14 and subtracting 6 from ⁻8 to get ⁻14.

Hooked!

15

14 13 12 11

2 3 4 5

1 6 7 8 9 10

0

-1 -6 -7 -8

-2 -3 -4 -5 -9

-10

-15

-14 -13 -12 -11

Dare!

Focus

Dare is a game for two or more players which practices adding and subtracting numbers to one decimal place.

What you need

▶ Playing cards

▶ Counters (a different colour for each player)

▶ Dare! game board

How to play

Firstly, the cards are shuffled and placed in a pile, face-down and within reach of all the players. The players' counters are placed on the number ten on the game board, which is the starting position. Player 1 takes a card and doubles its value. They must then divide this total by ten and subtract the answer from the value underneath their counter. If correct, they move their counter to the relevant number on the game board.

For Example

Player 1 picks up a six. They double it (to twelve), divide the answer by ten (to get 1.2), then subtract this amount from the number under their counter (10 – 1.2 = 8.8). Having found the correct answer, they move their counter to 8.8 on the game board.

After moving their counter, Player 1 must then decide whether to play safe, stop and pass the cards to the next player or to 'dare' and turn over another card. If Player 1 decides to dare and turn over another card then:

▶ if the card is the same colour they can continue their turn by performing the necessary calculation (doubling the value on the card, dividing it by ten and subtracting it from the number under their counter, in this case 8.8);

▶ if the card is a different colour they must go back to the first grey **DARE SQUARE** they reach by moving backwards along the game board.

If Player 1 decides to stop then play goes to Player 2. Play continues with players taking cards in turn, doubling its value, dividing by ten and subtracting this from the number underneath their counter.

Players are encouraged to do all their mental calculations before moving the counter. If a player lands on top of another counter, the counter landed on is moved back to the start or the first **DARE SQUARE** they reach by moving backwards along the game board, (whichever is agreed by the players before play).

How to win

The first player to land on or go past zero (the finish line) is the winner.

Rule changes / Next steps

▶ Remove the lower number cards (1—4) for practice subtracting larger numbers.

▶ Play as an addition game, starting at zero and adding up to the finish line.

▶ Each player starts with a blue dare counter and is allowed to use it once at any time during the game. The dare counter forces another player to dare and carry on even when they have decided to stop. The dared player *must* then carry on for two more cards.

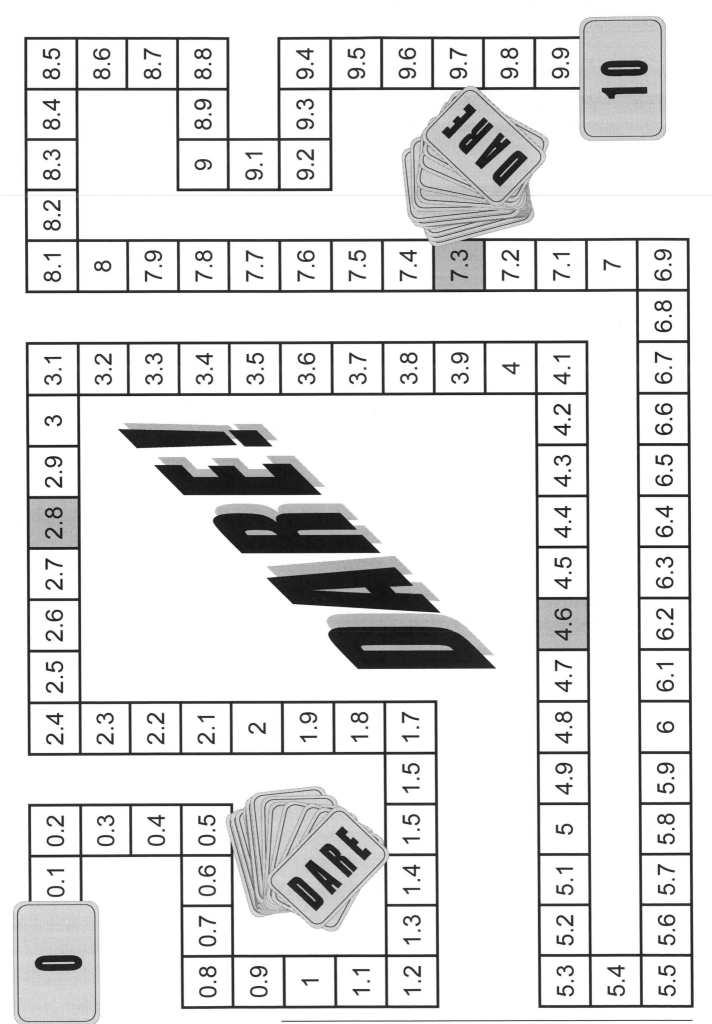

Speed Seekers

Focus

Speed Seekers is a game for two or more players which practices adding and subtracting numbers to one decimal place.

What you need

▶ Playing cards (aces to fours removed)

▶ Counters (a different colour for each player)

▶ Speed Seekers game board

How to play

The lower cards are removed from the pack and the remainder are shuffled and placed in a pile, face-down and within reach of all the players. Player 1 takes a card from the top of the pack and doubles its value to get a total. They then divide this total by ten and subtract their answer from the number underneath their counter on the game board, moving their counter to this new position.

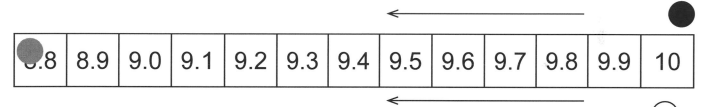

For example

Player 1 (grey counter) turns over a six. First of all they calculate double six (2 x 6 = 12). They divide by ten (12 ÷ 10 = 1.2) and subtract the answer from the number under their counter (10 – 1.2 = 8.8).

Play goes to Player 2, and play continues with players taking cards in turn, doubling them and then dividing by ten and subtracting this total from the number underneath their counter.

Players must do all their mental calculations before moving their counter. The player must also give the correct answer to move their counter otherwise it remains where it is on the game board.

If a player lands on a Speed Seeker (grey) square they can choose to either move another nine spaces or move any one other player backwards nine squares on the game board.

If a player lands on top of another counter, the counter landed on is moved back to the first Speed Seeker square they reach by moving backwards along the game board.

How to win

The first player to land on or go past zero (the finish line) on the game board is the winner.

Rule changes / Next steps

▶ Play as an addition game, starting at the lower number and adding up to the finish line.

▶ Remove cards eight and above and instead of doubling, players multiply the number by three before dividing the total by ten.

10

0

Speed Seekers

The Ten Dash

Focus

The Ten Dash is a game for two or more players which practices adding and subtracting numbers to one decimal place.

What you need

▶ Playing cards

▶ Counters (a different colour for each player)

▶ The Ten Dash game board

How to play

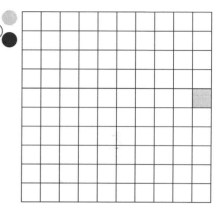

Firstly the cards are shuffled and then placed in a pile, face-down and within reach of all the players. Each player starts with a counter of their own colour at the start of the game board (first diagram).

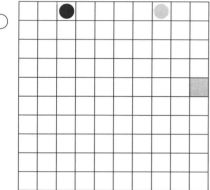

Player 1 starts the game by turning over a card and placing it face-up in front of them. They divide the number by ten and then move to that number on the game board.

For example

Player 1 (black counter) turns over a three. This is divided by ten $(3 \div 10 = 0.3)$ so Player 1 moves their counter to the matching number on the game board.

Player 2 (grey counter) then turns over an eight. This is divided by ten $(8 \div 10 = 0.8)$, so Player 2 moves to that number on the board.

Play continues in this fashion. If, for example, Player 1 turned over a nine on their next turn they would have to do $0.3 + 0.9 = 1.2$ and move to that position on the game board.

Players must do all their mental calculations before moving their counter. The player must also give the correct answer to move their counter, otherwise it remains in the same place on the game board.

If a player lands on top of another player's counter below five they send their opponent back to the start. If the counter is beyond five then it is sent back to that halfway square.

How to win

The first player to land on or go past ten (finish line) is the winner.

Rule changes / Next steps

▶ Start at ten, subtracting the value of the card multiplied by ten, with the finish line at zero.

▶ Players have a boost counter that they can play once in the game to double the number on their card. This could be played before or after the card is turned over.

▶ Encourage children to investigate patterns in adding and subtracting numbers, such as $15 - 6 = 9$ so $1.5 - 0.6 = 0.9$ and $0.15 - 0.06 = 0.09$.

The Ten Dash

0.1	0.2	0.3	0.4	0.5	0.6	0.7	0.8	0.9	1
1.1	1.2	1.3	1.4	1.5	1.6	1.7	1.8	1.9	2
2.1	2.2	2.3	2.4	2.5	2.6	2.7	2.8	2.9	3
3.1	3.2	3.3	3.4	3.5	3.6	3.7	3.8	3.9	4
4.1	4.2	4.3	4.4	4.5	4.6	4.7	4.8	4.9	5
5.1	5.2	5.3	5.4	5.5	5.6	5.7	5.8	5.9	6
6.1	6.2	6.3	6.4	6.5	6.6	6.7	6.8	6.9	7
7.1	7.2	7.3	7.4	7.5	7.6	7.7	7.8	7.9	8
8.1	8.2	8.3	8.4	8.5	8.6	8.7	8.8	8.9	9
9.1	9.2	9.3	9.4	9.5	9.6	9.7	9.8	9.9	10

Battle Squares

Focus

Battle Squares is a game for two or more players which practices dividing by ten and adding and subtracting numbers to one decimal place.

What you need

▶ Playing cards (tens and picture cards removed)

▶ Counters (a different colour for each player)

▶ Battle Squares game board

▶ Battle Squares scorecard

How to play

When the tens and picture cards have been removed from the pack the remaining cards are shuffled and placed in a pile, face-down and within reach of all the players.

Player 1 turns over two cards and uses them to make a two-digit number which they then divide by ten.

For example

If Player 1 turns over a 3 and a 7 they can either make the number 3.7 or 7.3. They must calculate how much more needs to be added to each number to make ten, whilst thinking about how many points they will get for placing a counter on a particular colour.

Player 1 may decide to calculate 3.7 + 6.3 = 10 and put a counter on 6.3 to score 0.5 points for a black square. However, if Player 1 decided to calculate 7.3 + 2.7 = 10 and put a counter on 2.7, they would score one point for a grey square.

Play continues with players taking it in turns to make two-digit numbers, divide them by ten, and calculate how many more to make ten. They then decide where to place their counters on the board to score the maximum number of points possible (players should watch out for dotty squares, which lose them points). Each player keeps their own score using a scorecard. Players must do all their mental calculations before placing their counter and must also give a correct answer in order to do so.

If a square is already covered by a counter then the player must switch their cards around to make the other two-digit number and must place their counter on the other available square. If both possible squares are covered then the player cannot place a counter but draws two new cards on their next turn. When all the cards have been used, shuffle them and place them in a pile, face-down, ready for the next player's turn.

How to win

The winner of the battle is the player with the most points after an agreed number of rounds.

Rule changes / Next steps

▶ Do calculations as subtraction from ten, such as 10 − 5.4 = 4.6 or 10 − 4.5 = 5.5.

▶ Players turn over three cards and can use any combination of them to make a two-digit number before dividing by ten.

▶ Play "in colour" : a full colour downloadable game board and scorecards are available on our website, www.tarquingroup.com.

BATTLE SQUARES

0.1	0.2	0.3	0.4	0.5	0.6	0.7	0.8	0.9	
1.1	1.2	1.3	1.4	1.5	1.6	1.7	1.8	1.9	S
2.1	2.2	2.3	2.4	2.5	2.6	2.7	2.8	2.9	Q
3.1	3.2	3.3	3.4	3.5	3.6	3.7	3.8	3.9	U
4.1	4.2	4.3	4.4	4.5	4.6	4.7	4.8	4.9	A
5.1	5.2	5.3	5.4	5.5	5.6	5.7	5.8	5.9	R
6.1	6.2	6.3	6.4	6.5	6.6	6.7	6.8	6.9	E
7.1	7.2	7.3	7.4	7.5	7.6	7.7	7.8	7.9	S
8.1	8.2	8.3	8.4	8.5	8.6	8.7	8.8	8.9	
	B	A	T	T	L	E			10

Full colour game board and scorecards downloadable from: www.tarquingroup.com.

Game Board © Tarquin Photocopiable under licence – for terms see page 2

BATTLE SQUARES SCORECARD

☐ = 0.2 points   ■ =0.5 points   ▤ = 2 points

▨ = 1 point   ▦ = -0.9 points

Keep your score like this:

Round Number	Points for square	Total Game points
1	stripes, 2 points	2
2	dotty, -0.9	2 - 0.9 = 1.1
3	grey, 1	1 + 1.1 = 2.1

Round Number	Points for square	Total Game points
1		
2		
3		
4		
5		
6		
7		
8		
9		
10		
11		
12		
13		
14		
15		

Flamingo Bingo

Focus

Flamingo Bingo is a game for two or more players which practices using a range of efficient mental methods for numbers up to fifty.

What you need

▶ Playing cards

▶ Counters

▶ Flamingo Bingo cards

▶ Whiteboard / paper and pen

How to play

Each player needs to start the game with a Flamingo Bingo card, eight counters and a whiteboard or paper and pen. The cards are shuffled and placed in a pile, face-down and within reach of all the players. Player 1 starts the game by turning over three cards. All players then use these three numbers in different ways, using addition, subtraction, multiplication and division, to try and make a number on their game card.

For example

Player 1 turns over a four, a two and a seven. Different numbers can be made as follows:

4 + 2 = 6	7 − 4 = 3	7 + 4 + 2 = 13
24 − 7 = 17	7 x 4 = 28	2 x 7 = 14
4 x 2 + 7 = 15	74 ÷ 2 = 37	42 ÷ 7 = 6

Players need to write down their calculation on paper or a whiteboard to show how they made the number on their bingo card and then cover it with a counter. A time limit of ten, twenty or thirty seconds needs to be placed on players to make a number. A player can only place one counter for each round. If a player can't think of a way to make an uncovered number, they can't place a counter for that round.

Play continues with players taking turns to put three cards face-up for all players to try and make another number on their card.

How to win

Players have to achieve a 'full house' by covering every number on their card. The first player to stand on one leg and shout 'Flamingo Bingo' (not compulsory!) is the winner. Player's calculations are checked at the end of the game to make sure they are correct.

Rule changes / Next steps

▶ Have one player as a referee who turns over cards and checks answers. Play as a whole class by having one bingo card between two or use the spare cards to make one each.

▶ Turn over four or five cards and give the players five minutes to try and make all the numbers on their bingo card by using only this one set of numbers.

Card 1

3	11			15
20	26			
38	45			49

Card 2

1			9	16
23				29
37	40			44

Card 3

			5	14
17			22	30
33		38	46	

Card 4

2	8			15
21	24			
36	39			47

Card 5

4				10
16	25			29
32			37	43

Card 6

7				13
19	23			28
35			44	50

Card 7

6	12			15
24				27
31	40			48

Card 8

2	7			
14	21			26
33	39			45

Card 9

2	14			17
25	28			34
	42			49

Card 10

5				9
16	20			22
37	41			48

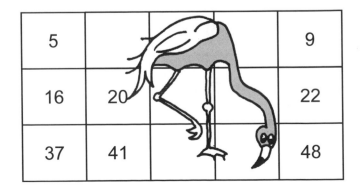

End of the Line

Focus

End of the Line is a game for two to four players which can be used to practice a range of efficient mental methods with numbers up to one hundred.

What you need

▶ Playing cards

▶ Counters (a different colour for each player)

▶ End of the Line game board

▶ Whiteboard / paper and pen

How to play

Player 1 turns over two cards from the top of the pack and places them next to each other. They must then look to see if they can make a multiple of six, seven, or eight (depending which track on the game board is being played) by adding, subtracting multiplying or even dividing the numbers on the cards.

 For example (using game board track 1: multiples of six up to 72)
Player 1 turns over an eight and a five as shown. Player 1 is not able to make a multiple of six using these cards. Play passes to Player 2, who turns over another card and tries to make a multiple of six using any or all three of the numbers on the cards.

 With a three, Player 2 can now make a multiple of six by calculating

3 x 8 = 24 or 8 – 5 + 3 = 6.

Player 2 decides to remove the eight and the three from the line and covers the matching multiple of twenty-four on the top row of the game board with a counter of their colour.

 Player 3 then turns over another card but as it is a ten they are unable to make a multiple of six and it becomes the turn of Player 4 to add a card to the line. Player 4 turns over a king and makes a multiple of six by calculating 13 + 10 – 5 = 18. Player 4 uses all three cards, so removes them and places a counter on eighteen on the game board.

The next player turns over two new cards and starts the line again. Play continues with players taking it in turns to place cards in the line and attempting to make multiples of six (or whichever muliples are being played) that have not been covered by a counter. A time limit can be set for players to make a multiple and if they can't do it in that time the next player has their turn.

How to win

The winner is the player with the most counters on the line when the last multiple is covered.

Rule changes / Next steps

▶ Play the game using any of the different sets of multiples on the game board or have a go at playing two different sets of multiples at the same time.

▶ Allow players to put cards together to make a two-digit number, such as a three and a four to make thirty-four or forty-three.

6	12	18	24	30	36	42	48	54	60	66	72

7	14	21	28	35	42	49	56	63	70	77	84

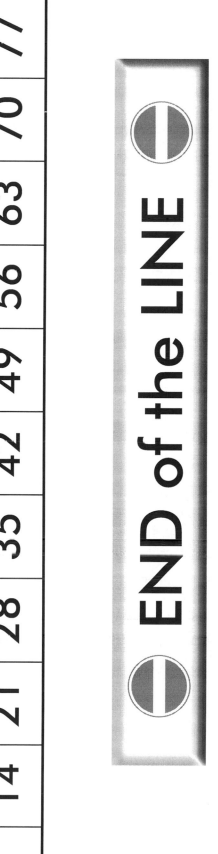

END of the LINE

8	16	24	32	40	48	56	64	72	80	88	96

Cover Up

Focus

Cover Up is a game for two to four players which can be used to practice a range of efficient mental methods with numbers up to one hundred.

What you need

▶ Playing cards (picture cards removed)

▶ Counters

▶ Cover Up game board

How to play

The picture cards are removed from the pack. The cards are shuffled, three cards are dealt to each player and the remaining cards are placed in a pile, face-down and within reach of all the players. Players must then look at their cards and try to find ways of making a multiple of any number on their row.

For example

Player 1 receives these cards and could use them to make any of the following possible numbers:

$8 \times 3 = 24$ (multiple of 3, 4, 6 and 8)
$68 - 3 = 65$ (multiple of 5)
$6 \times 8 = 48$ (multiple of 3, 4, 6 and 8)
$6 \times 8 - 3 = 45$ (multiple of 3, 5 and 9)

Player 1 choses to say $6 \times 8 - 3 = 45$, and chooses 9 as a factor of 45, and so places a counter on the number 9 in their row.

The other players must check that the answers are correct, and if so Player 1 can place a counter onto the number on their row. Player 1 then picks up two or three more cards from the top of the pack to replace the cards they used, and starts looking to see if they can make a number for their next turn.

Play continues with players taking it in turns to put cards down to try and make different answers. Only one number can be covered with a counter on each turn. If a player can't make a number on their row they can choose to change one, two or all three of their cards instead. They place the cards they don't want on the bottom of the central pile and take the same number of new cards from the top. However, this exchange of cards counts as the player's turn: they are not allowed to try to place a counter. When the cards in the middle run out the next player picks up all those in front of each player, shuffles them and places them back face-down in a pile again.

How to win

The first player to cover all the numbers on their row with a counter is the winner.

Rule changes / Next steps

▶ Players must use all three cards on every turn.

▶ If a player can make a square number with the cards, then as well as placing a counter on their own Cover Up row they can also remove any one counter from another player's row.

▶ Make links between multiples and factors. For example, eighteen is a multiple of 1, 2, 3, 6, 9 and 18 so all these numbers are factors of 18.

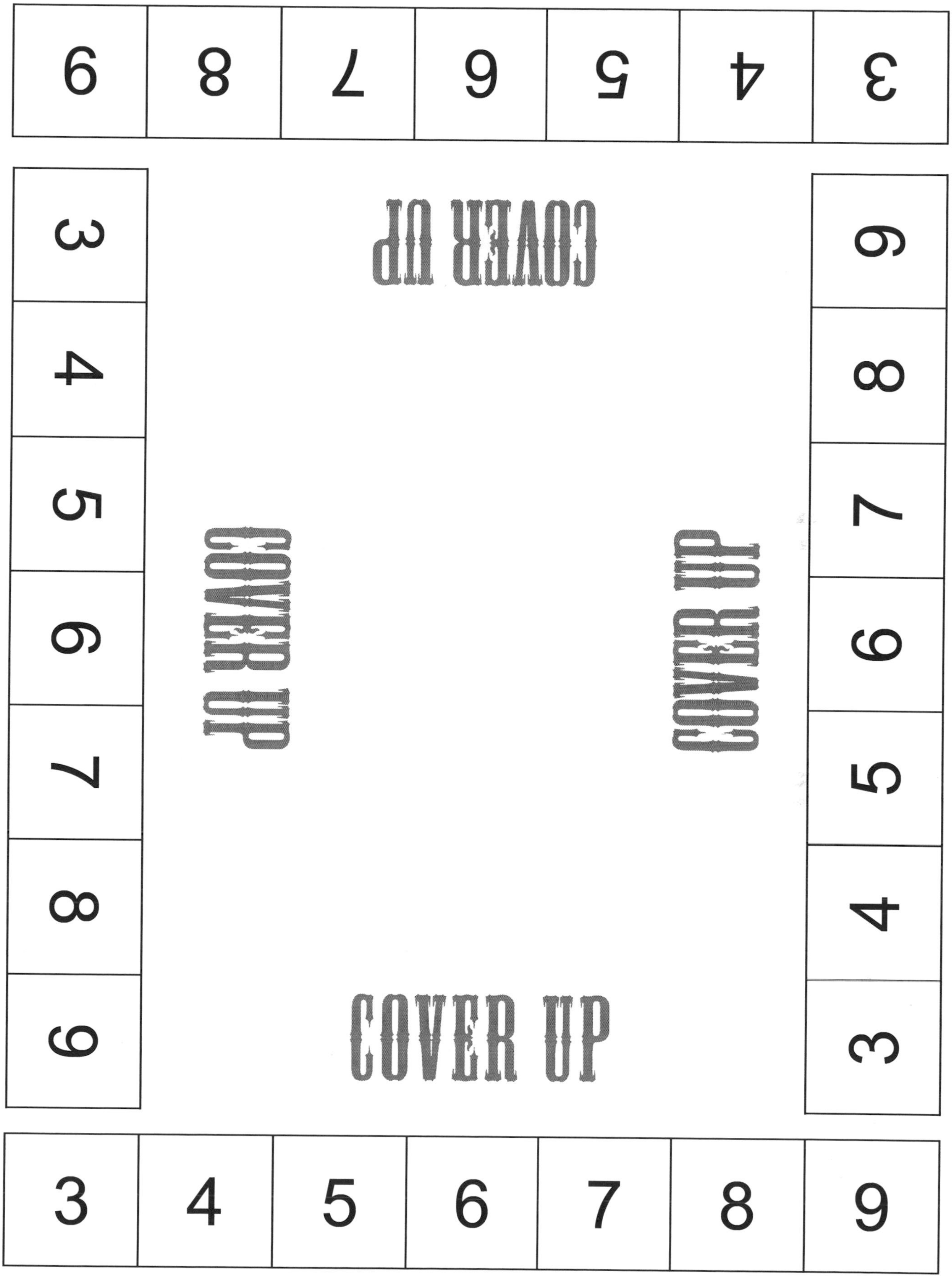
COVER UP
3 4 5 6 7 8 9

Quads

Focus

Quads is a game for three or more players which can be used to practice a range of efficient mental methods with numbers up to one thousand and to one decimal place.

What you need

▶ Playing cards

▶ Counters (a different colour for each player)

▶ Quads game board

How to play

Player 1 turns over any number of cards and could be asked to add, subtract or multiply them to get an answer depending on what skill or knowledge from the Year 5 programme of study the game is being used to practice. If the player gets the answer correct they can place a counter of their own colour in a circle on the game board.

Player 2 then turns over one or more cards and performs a similar calculation. They can place a counter of their colour onto the game board if the answer is correct, but if they answer incorrectly they are not able to place a counter on that turn. Play continues in this way with players taking it in turns to take one or more cards, answer questions and place counters on the game board.

How to win

The first player to make a Quad is the winner. Quads can be a rectangle or in a straight line (vertical, horizontal or diagonal) as shown in the diagram. Rectangles formed can be small or large and can appear in any orientation.

Remove all the counters and play again.

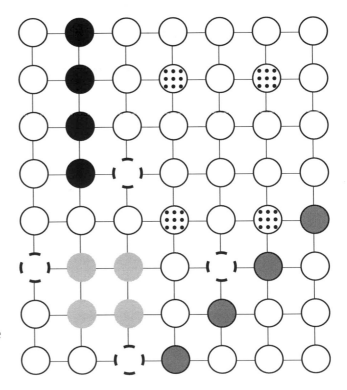

Rule changes / Next steps

▶ Players continue to try and make Quads until all the spaces are covered or until the players agree that no more can be made. Players score four points for every Quad they make and the winner is the player with the most points at the end of the game.

▶ Restrict players to making only rectangles or straight lines to win the game rather than allowing both.

QUADS

Monster Mash-Up

Focus

Monster Mash-up is a game for two to six players which can be used to practice a range of efficient mental methods with numbers up to one million and to two decimal places.

What you need

▶ Playing cards (cards 1–5)

▶ Counters (one for each player)

▶ Monster Mash-Up game board

▶ Question cards, if using (see Next Steps, below)

How to play

When the cards from six upwards have been removed from the pack the remaining cards are shuffled and placed in a pile, face-down and within reach of all the players. Players then choose a monster and place their counter on it, ready for the start of the game.

Player 1 is asked a question by the question master to practice recall of facts or any skill within the Year 5 programme of study. If answered correctly Player 1 turns over a card and can then move the same number of spaces on the game board. If the answer is incorrect the player is not allowed to move their counter. The other players are then asked questions in turn. If correct they can turn over a card and move the same number of spaces on the game board.

Black holes and transporters

Players must try and avoid the black holes in various positions on the game board, since landing on one sends them back to 'their' monster at the start of the game. However, if a player lands on a black hole containing a symbol, they must transport themselves to any other black hole with the same symbol on it.

Players are allowed to move between tracks and go anywhere on the board, though can't keep moving backwards and forwards from one square to another. If a player lands on top of another counter, the counter landed on is moved back to any monster of that player's choosing.

How to win

The first player to land on or go beyond an end square is the winner.

Rule changes / Next steps

▶ Players can move one bonus square if they can answer a question that another player has answered incorrectly.

▶ Different kinds of question may be selected, dependent, for example, on what a particular child needs to practice, or on particular skills needed for assessment purposes.

▶ Players must turn the exact number to land on an end square and win the game.

▶ Use the set of mixed mental questions provided. Put them face-down on the table for children to pick at random, read aloud and then answer. Alternatively, pass them to an appointed question master to read out.

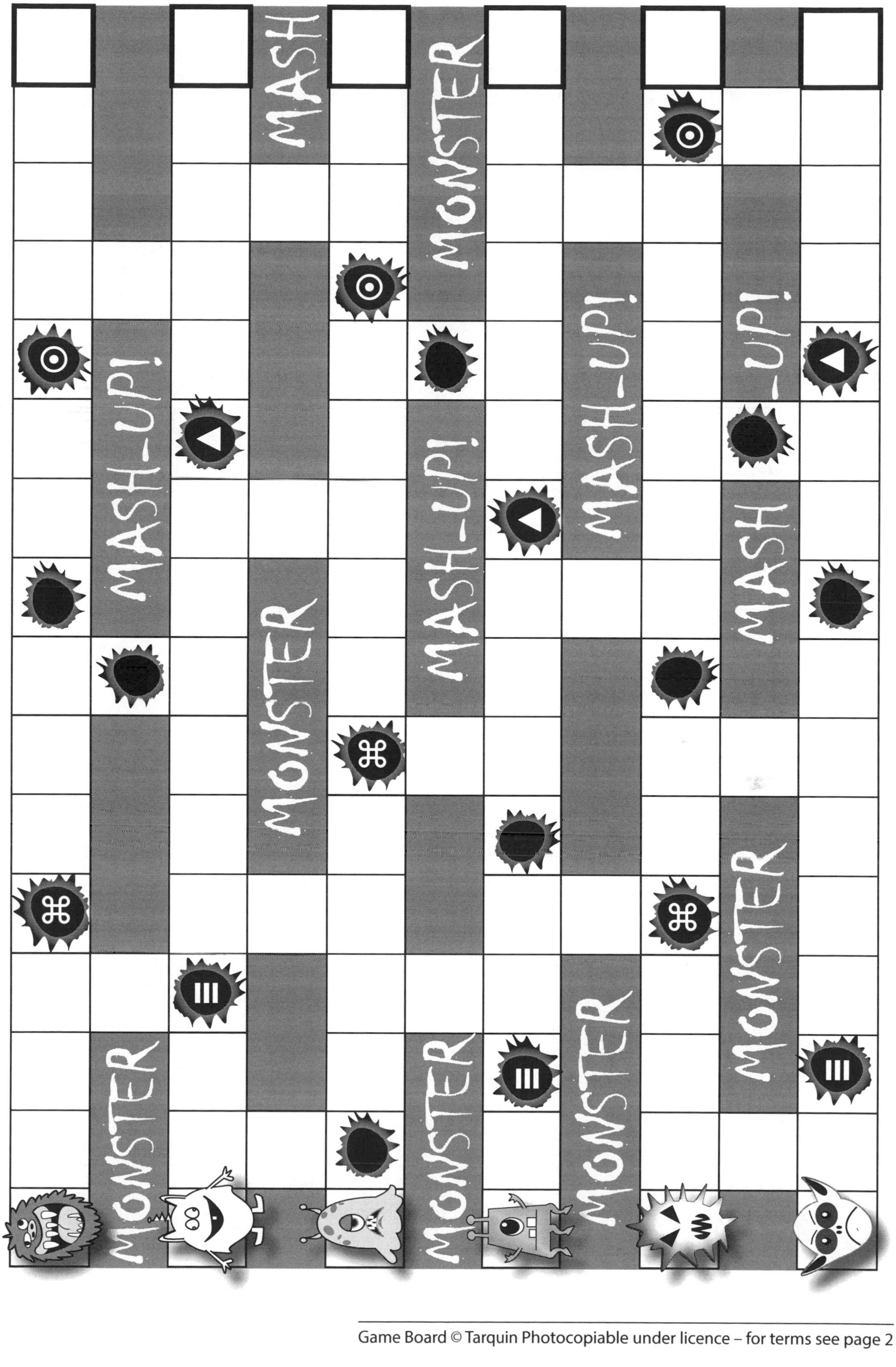

What are the two missing numbers? … , 1.8, 1.5, 1.2, …	What are the two missing numbers? …, 6½, 6, 5½, 5, …	What is 900 more than 9890?	What is 2500 less than 30 000?
What is 10 000 more than 99 420?	What is 10 000 less than 106 758?	What is the 6 worth in 376 280?	What is the value of the underlined digit in 542 183?
True or False 100 066 > 97 458	True or False 623 001 < 591 994	Write the number six hundred and twenty thousand one hundred and eight in figures.	Write the number eight hundred and thirty thousand and fifty in figures.
24 081 = 20 000 + 3000 + ___	945 146 = 900 000 + _____ + 15 146	What is 935 286 rounded to the nearest 10 000?	What is 706 423 rounded to the nearest 1000?
What is 35 756 rounded to the nearest 10?	What is 48 050 rounded to the nearest 100?	CLXX =	MMXIV =
37 248 + 3060 =	61 503 − 240 =	70 620 + 6900 =	604 000 − 1360
580 + 730	11 200 − 8400	10 000 = __ + 2900	4500 = 6200 − __
__ + 4500 = 20 100	__ − 7000 = 4800	What is the sum of 68 000 and 5300?	What is the difference between 7140 and 6950?

13 x 6 =	5 x 80 =	12 x 9 =	600 x 7 =
40 x 11 =	40 x 90 =	640 ÷ 8 =	240 ÷ 30 =
Name all the factors of 36.	What is the next prime number after 13?	If 5 x 12 = 60, what is 50 x 120?	If 9 x 9 = 81, what is 90 x 90?
56 = __ x 8	__ ÷ 90 = 5	4 = 48 ÷ __	6 x __ = 54
What is two sixths of 24?	What is three ninths of 72?	One eighth of a number is 4. What is the number?	I think of a number and find one fifth. The answer is 50. What is the number?
True or False 50% > ¼	True or False 0.8 = ⅛	What is the decimal equivalent of one fifth?	What is the fraction equivalent of 0.7?
What is ⅜ of 400?	What is ⅔ of 60?	What is ⅞ + ⅜?	What is 2⅓ - ⅔?
What is 9.65 rounded to the nearest whole number?	What is 3.05 rounded to the nearest tenth?	Write 2⅞ as an improper fraction.	How many sixths are there in two and a half?

Tarquin Mathematics Resources

Tarquin has more than a thousand product lines to support and enrich mathematics. You can browse them at **www.tarquingroup.com**.

To make it easy to buy what you need to really use this book, we have some special packages online — put the keyword ACE into the quick search box to see the full range at once.

▶ Packs of Playing Cards

▶ Coloured Counters

▶ Beads

Other Tarquin Products designed for you

Books

First Tables Colouring Book

Second Tables Colouring Book

Arithmetic Arithmetic

Tables Cubes

Mathematical Vocabulary 2

The Week's Problem

A Puzzle a Day

Junior Mathematical Team Games

Junior Mini Mathematical Murder Mysteries

Posters

One Million Poster

Multiples Poster

Equal Parts Poster

Quadrilaterals and Polygons Poster

Roman Numerals Poster

Dice and other Manipulatives

Excellent prices on 12-sided and 10-sided dice classroom packs — ideal for mental mathematics.

Tarquin, Suite 74, 17 Holywell Hill, St Albans, AL1 1DT
Tel: +44 (0)1727833866 Fax: +44 (0)845 456 6385
www.tarquingroup.com   Follow us on Twitter @TarquinGroup